# Einstein's God

## A Way - of Being Spiritual
## Without the Supernatural

Todd Macalister

apocryphile press
BERKELEY, CA


Apocryphile Press
1700 Shattuck Ave #81
Berkeley, CA 94709
www.apocryphile.org

© 2008 by Todd Macalister
All rights reserved

Photo of Einstein courtesy of the Library of Congress Prints
and Photographs Division Washington, D.C. 20540 USA.
Galaxy photo courtesy of NASA's Hubble Site, http://hubblesite.org/

Printed in the United States of America
ISBN 1-933993-65-0

# Contents

| | |
|---|---|
| Preface | i |
| Introduction | iii |
| Einstein's God | 1 |
| The Way of Science | 13 |
| Ways of Sensing the Divine | 17 |
| A Choice | 25 |
| A New Kind of Faith | 41 |
| A New Kind of Religion | 47 |
| Postscript | 57 |
| Notes | 59 |
| Bibliography | 73 |

# Preface

After years of attending, I stepped away from the church.

The stories seemed impossible – an all-knowing presence, invisible angels, and fiery pits of hell . . . I couldn't believe it. And it didn't make sense to just go along.

I knew that *something* lay behind the beauty and order in all we see. But, my sense of this needed to fit with what seems real.

Millions, around the world, share this view. And, as we recognize forces greater than ourselves but reject the supernatural, many of us see ourselves, as Albert Einstein did, as "deeply religious nonbelievers".

But, in rejecting the traditional, we are on our own. We have no bible to learn from, and no church or community.

We need a new way of framing what we understand and feel. And we need words that can help us consider what we believe.

# Introduction

> "Einstein was a giant.
> His head was in the clouds,
> but his feet were on the ground."
>
> Richard Feynman

Albert Einstein was a modern prophet. He didn't believe in a personal God. But, with reverence for the force that lies behind the order in our world, he pointed to a new kind of faith.

This book begins with quotes that give an overview of Einstein's spiritual views. It shows how a world-view grounded in science can serve as a basis for reverence. And it shows how core elements in religions - hope and faith - can be gained with Einstein's God. This book examines parallels between Einstein's views and traditional systems of belief. It looks at ways of gaining from both the old and the new, but it also identifies a choice that must be made.

So, if traditional faiths don't fit with what you see -

if you see yourself as "spiritual, but not religious",

if you attend services, but only partially believe,

or if you think you're not really spiritual at all -

take a look.

You may find something you can say you _do_ believe.

# Einstein's God

After establishing himself as a scientist, Albert Einstein's views were sought on many topics. He spoke frequently about religion, and described a way of being spiritual that does not include belief in the supernatural. He said . . .

> I am a deeply religious nonbeliever....
> This is a somewhat new kind of religion.

I cannot conceive of a personal God
who would directly influence
the actions of individuals,
or would directly sit in judgment
on creatures of his own creation. . .




There is nothing divine about morality;
it is a purely human affair.




I do not believe in immortality.

Mere unbelief in a personal God
is no philosophy at all.

Everyone who is seriously involved
in the pursuit of science
becomes convinced that
a spirit is manifest
in the laws of the Universe -
a spirit vastly superior to that of man,
and one in the face of which
we with our modest powers
must feel humble.

You will hardly find one
among the profounder sort of scientific minds
without a religious feeling of his own.
But it is different from the religiosity
of the naive man.

For the latter,
God is a being
from whose care one hopes to benefit
and whose punishment one fears;
a sublimation of a feeling
similar to that of a child for its father,
a being to whom one stands, so to speak,
in a personal relation,
however deeply it may be tinged with awe.

But the scientist is possessed
by the sense of universal causation. . .
His religious feeling takes the form
of a rapturous amazement
at the harmony of natural law,
which reveals an intelligence
of such superiority
that, compared with it,
all the systematic thinking
and acting of human beings
is an utterly insignificant reflection. . .

It is . . . a feeling of awe
at the scheme that is manifested
in the material universe. . .
There is in this neither a will
nor a goal, nor a must,
but only sheer being.

If something is in me
which can be called religious
then it is the unbounded admiration
for the structure of the world
so far as our science can reveal it.

I cannot conceive of a God
who rewards and punishes his creatures,
or has a will of the type of which
we are conscious in ourselves.
An individual
who should survive his physical death
is also beyond my comprehension,
nor do I wish it otherwise . . .
Enough for me
the mystery of the eternity of life,
and the inkling
of the marvelous structure of reality,
together with the single-hearted endeavor
to comprehend a portion,
be it never so tiny,
of the reason that manifests itself in nature.

My religion consists
of a humble admiration
of the illimitable superior spirit
who reveals himself in the slight details
we are able to perceive
with our frail and feeble minds.
That deeply emotional conviction
of the presence
of a superior reasoning power,
which is revealed
in the incomprehensible Universe,
forms my idea of God.

I believe in Spinoza's God
who reveals Himself
in the orderly harmony of what exists,
not in a God
who concerns himself
with fates and actions of human beings.


I believe in the brotherhood of man
and the uniqueness of the individual.

The fairest thing we can experience
is the mysterious.

It is the fundamental emotion
which stands at the cradle of true art
and true science.
He who knows it not
and can no longer wonder,
no longer feel amazement,
is as good as dead, a snuffed-out candle.

It was the experience of mystery -
even if mixed with fear -
that engendered religion.
A knowledge of the existence
of something we cannot penetrate,
of the manifestations
of the profoundest reason
and the most radiant beauty,
which are only accessible to our reason
in their most elementary forms -
it is this knowledge
and this emotion
that constitute the truly religious attitude;

in this sense, and in this alone,
I am a deeply religious man.

# The Way of Science

> "The further the spiritual evolution of mankind advances, the more certain it seems to me that the path to genuine religiosity does not lie through the fear of life, and the fear of death, and blind faith, but through striving after rational knowledge."
>
> Albert Einstein

Einstein's religion combined a spiritual sense with a world-view grounded in science. He had an emotional response, with reverence and awe, when he considered the wonders of creation. But, he recognized we know nothing about the force that brought this all into being.

> "We are in the position of a little child
> entering a huge library
> filled with books in many different languages.
> The child knows that someone
> must have written those books.
> It does not know how.
> It does not understand the languages
> in which they are written.
> The child dimly suspects a mysterious order
> in the arrangement of the books
> but it does not know what it is.
> That, it seems to me, is the attitude
> of even the most intelligent human being toward God."

He saw nature as an expression of the force that guides our world. And he felt that, as we begin to understand small parts of what is, we may get a glimpse - some insight - into the force that causes all things to be as they are.

Einstein felt that the attempt to understand expresses a type of reverence. And he felt that the goal and method of science - "striving after rational knowledge" - could be a Way of spiritual practice and seeking.

With this approach, we observe, then form an idea.

> Then we challenge and test the idea - to see if it holds true.

When a view holds up - we accept it.

> But, if we learn something new or find a better way of explaining, we revise the view to match our understanding.

This fits with several Eastern views, which see knowledge as a path to enlightenment.

> But, it differs from basing beliefs on ancient revelations, as written in holy books.

> It differs from belief in what one simply *feels* is true.

> And, it is different from the type of faith that celebrates maintaining belief - even when evidence suggests it may be false.

Einstein considered, but could not accept, many concepts in traditional religion - a personal god, miracles, and life after death. He recognized the appeal of these. And he knew it was not possible to disprove them. But, apart from their mythic/symbolic truth, nothing in our understanding of the world explains how they could be.

He saw the world as wholly based in natural laws. And, while he recognized that this, also, could not be proven, it fit with all the evidence he had, and all he could understand. As his best sense of what is - how things seem to be - it served as a type of belief.

He didn't speculate on what he felt was unknowable.

"I don't try to imagine a God . . ."

Instead, he felt . . .

" . . . it suffices to stand in awe of the structure of the world, insofar as it allows our inadequate senses to appreciate it."

This approach has several virtues.

It is noble.

It seeks the truth.

It is honest,
> in describing things as best we understand them, not as we wish them to be.

It is humble.
> It acknowledges there are many things that we do not understand.

And, by offering a spiritual framework, it can avoid the mental conflicts - the need to struggle to believe, or disbelieve, or suspend disbelief - that come when beliefs and rational knowledge are not in accord.

A rational view is not the only way of understanding. But, it is a core part of what makes us human. And, for some, this way of thinking is so strong that we cannot ignore it when we consider matters of faith.

As Einstein saw, and as is discussed throughout this book, a scientific view can include deep spiritual feelings. And it offers images - of ourselves and our world - that are as majestic, revealing, and mysterious as ancient myth.

> Where once the Earth seemed the center of all,
> we now see a vast and ancient cosmos.
>
> With the perspectives of Darwin and biology,
> we have a deeper understanding the wonder of life
> and the kinship of all living things.
>
> Where once we feared demonic possession,
> we now look at the brain to understand mental illness.

But many things, with this perspective, are not very different from systems that worship a personal god. Both views recognize that

> forces beyond our control affect our lives,
>
> and as we face personal and social challenges, we need standards (ways of determining what is right) and sources of wisdom and strength.

The Way of Science plays a critical role in values. It also offers a clear basis for reverence. For, the more we understand, the more we are impressed with the order and beauty in our world.

This approach is not for everyone. Different beliefs and ways of seeking suit different people.

But, for those who are inclined to question traditional beliefs and are unsatisfied by the answers they receive, it can offer a framework in which a deep spiritual sense can be embraced with both heart and mind.

# Ways of Sensing the Divine

> "Everyone who is seriously involved in the pursuit of science
> becomes convinced that
> a spirit is manifest in the laws of the Universe -
> a spirit vastly superior to that of man,
> and one in the face of which
> we with our modest powers must feel humble."
>
> Albert Einstein

Science-based views have been criticized as limited and unfeeling. By offering logic and data and theories, they may appear to be just an analysis of facts.

But, while science requires a rational check on what is believed, it has also confirmed the value of faith and the presence of things we cannot touch or see. Like Einstein, many with science-based views have deep spiritual feelings. And, while the object they are directed toward may differ from traditional religions, the nature and depth of these feelings have much in common.

> We may lose ourselves in music, the beauty of a flower, or the sparkle of sunlight on water.
>
> When a child is born, we are moved by the wonder of life.
>
> Some have mystical moments - of insight or love, or a sense of oneness with all that is.

These may spark a sense of something sacred. They point to another dimension - a non-material reality - in a spirituality that fits with science.

## A spirit in things

Einstein felt that something - a "spirit", he called it - lies behind and is expressed in all we see. He didn't see this as a supernatural presence. Instead, he recognized a vital force that set the cosmos in motion and causes all things to be as they are.

We are familiar with many types of spirits.

> One is the spirit we sense in living things - a distinctive personality or presence. This begins at conception, then grows and matures. And, at the moment of death, it is gone. When it is present, we recognize a life force. And, when it passes, something lingers - in our thoughts and dreams, and in the air, in a shared mood where all remember.
>
> Another is a spirit of place - a particular mood we may feel - in a pine grove, on a familiar road, or by a stream or a misty field or a special rock. When ancients recognized this, they often felt that wood nymphs, fairies, river spirits, or other beings were present.
>
> Another is a spirit in emotions or ideas - like the spirit of Christmas, a spirit of patriotism, or a spirit of compassion or love.

In all of these, something intangible forms an impression, and we have a sense of some type of presence. And, since this presence can often affect how we feel, these spirits are very real.

## A sense of belonging

We may have a sense of belonging - what some might describe as feeling the love and presence of God.

This can be a simple thing - a sense of comfort, a mood of calm contentment - of fitting in and not being alone.

It may include a sense of brotherhood - with strangers, family, and friends.

Or, in a more rare and dramatic expression, this may rise to a mystical sense of oneness - timeless and transcendent. As one person described this . . .

> "I had the sense that I was
> intimately connected to everything -
> the sky, the trees, the grass, . . . the garden walls.
> It was as if everything in the universe
> was in its proper place. . . .
> I was filled with a sense of peacefulness
> that I had never known before."

## A sense of something more . . .

We may also have more specific sensations.

We may hear a voice, or have a vision.

We may have a sense that someone, or something, is near.

These types of perceptions have been a key part of moments of revelation - for historical religious figures, and for everyday believers. They may also occur in more commonplace ways - in moments of *deja vu*, in dreams, or when an answer - a flash of insight - announces itself in a clear and certain voice. They may occur in schizophrenia and some types of epilepsy, and in high fever and some other physical states.

When seen from a Judeo-Christian perspective, these may be seen as messages from God.

In some ancient traditions and New Age views, they may be seen as ghosts or fairies, angels or demons - a pantheon of invisible beings.

In the modern scientific view, these perceptions originate in our brains.

Modern psychology recognizes the subconscious as a rich, creative realm where, in dreams and daydreams, with metaphoric images and imagination, we may have fantastic thoughts or perceptions. And, medical literature has many examples of hallucinations and mystical sensations being triggered by brain activity.

For example, the Russian writer, Fyodor Dostoevsky described a type of epilepsy that could cause an ecstatic feeling before a seizure.

"For several instants I experience a happiness that is impossible in an ordinary state, and of which other people have no conception. I feel full harmony in myself and in the whole world, and the feeling is so strong and sweet that for a few seconds of such bliss one could give up ten years of life, perhaps all of life. I felt that heaven descended to earth and swallowed me . . .

All of you healthy people don't even suspect what happiness is, that happiness that we epileptics experience for a second before an attack."

Stimulation of certain brain areas can trigger perceptions or feelings. When a mild electrical current was delivered to the temporal lobe (in epilepsy patients, prior to surgery), many reported hearing voices - sometimes close and clear, sometimes far away and difficult to understand. Some heard music, or shouting, or felt afraid.

These types of sensations may also occur in "normal" situations. For example, the psychologist, Julian Jaynes, described a personal experience - where, when seeking a solution to a problem, he heard an answer.

> "Suddenly, out of an absolute quiet, there came a firm, distinct loud voice from my upper right . . . It lugged me to my feet absurdly exclaiming, 'Hello?' looking for whoever was in the room. The voice had had an exact location. No one was there! Not even behind the wall where I sheepishly looked."

He described others who had similar experiences, and concluded that, while he did not consider the voice he heard to have been divinely inspired,

> "I do think that it is similar to what was heard by those who have in the past claimed such special selection."

People vary in the extent to which they experience these types of perceptions.

Some may have an occasional or once-in-a-lifetime event.

Many others never experience such a thing and, apart from insanity, they cannot conceive of it as possible.

And, for some, these may be commonplace occurrences.

The frequency seems to vary in different cultures. Stress and related factors may serve as triggers.

Jaynes felt that these voices originate in the brain, and that "... experiencing them is just like hearing an actual sound."

Others have taken this further, in recognizing the brain as determining the nature of what we perceive - regardless of where a stimulus arises. In this view . . .

> If God exists and speaks to us -
> we receive a message in brain areas that process sound.
> Then, we interpret the words, are conscious of the communication, and may feel comfort or awe or other emotions.

Or, if a rare or abnormal signal in our brain causes us to hear a voice -
> we receive a message in brain areas that process sound.
> Then, we interpret the words, are conscious of the communication, and may feel comfort or awe or other emotions.

In both cases, the same type of brain activity is required to receive, interpret, and respond to the message.

It may be difficult to distinguish perceptions that originate as something outside of us - something "real" - from those that originate in our brains. But, in some important ways, it doesn't matter.

> These types of feelings may be beautiful or frightening.

> They can have power and meaning.

> They can be among the most memorable and important events in peoples' lives.

> They are part of being human, and are a core element in what has moved people - in all cultures and times - to recognize "something more", and form ways of interpreting this and worshipping it in religion.

Whether they originate in our brains, or from supernatural beings, these types of perceptions put us in a place that is special and different. They give a sense that there is more than we are able to touch and see - something magical, something that may be beautiful and wise, and something that may seem more attractive than daily reality.

Having these feelings can be seen as a blessing, a state of grace. And those who have experienced it often seek it out again. As students and seekers, as monks or regular practitioners - many people are moved by these feelings to an extent that they are a driving force in their lives, giving purpose and direction and, for a number of people, something to spend a lifetime studying and striving toward.

Brain activity in spiritual states has become an active area of study. Researchers have identified areas of the brain that become active or quiet in the deepest states of meditation. They are learning how emotions occur, how we may feel connected with others, and how drugs and disease can affect what we feel.

Researchers have also learned that we sometimes have a strong sense of things that are not actually there (as in the circles that seem to appear in the image below).

And, as in shapes in clouds, or constellations in the sky, or the illusion of a square (below), we see familiar patterns in unrelated objects or events.

Many additional insights are expected. But, regardless of how much we learn, it is likely that a gap - a major mystery - will remain, in our inability to even begin to understand how patterns of nerve cell and chemical activity in our brains become the thoughts we perceive in our minds and what we feel in our hearts and souls.

A science-based view includes a recognition that some of what we sense and feel - things that, in important ways, are real -

    are more than material reality.

But, it also, assumes that, unless a clear external source can be found, these are more likely to have originated from processes that are known to occur - in our brains - than from contact with supernatural beings.

# A Choice

"The main source of the present-day conflicts between the spheres of religion and science lies in the concept of a personal God."

Albert Einstein

Insights from science have led to fundamental changes in how we see ourselves and our world. They have enabled us to live healthier, more comfortable, and increasingly longer lives. But, since they often conflict with tradition, new views have shaken belief in some, prompted responses from churches, and caused uncertainty and dissension.

There's no avoiding what's been learned - no turning back. But, there's also a sense that, just because some aspects of our understanding have changed, it would be foolish to reject ancient wisdom.

There is also a recognition that science does not attempt to address many topics that are core parts of religion. These include personal and social challenges - sources of guidance, sources of hope and strength, and ways of coping with loss and mortality.

Here, we seek wisdom, rather than knowledge. And we think toward what could be, rather than just examining what is.

## Trying to have it both ways

An attempt at compromise has been made in the relationship between science and religion. This looks to the best of what each has to offer, and assigns a place of value for each.

Stephen Jay Gould described this as "non-overlapping magesteria" (NOMA). Here, the focus of science is facts (what is), while religion examines what is right, what is good, and what should be.

This view has been present since at least the time of Galileo who, in his trial before the inquisition, quoted Cardinal Baronius's statement - that the Bible "is intended to teach us how to go to heaven, not how the heavens go."

Einstein echoed this in a famous statement:

> "The scientific method can teach us nothing else
> beyond how facts are related to,
> and conditioned by, each other. . .
> Yet it is equally clear that
> knowledge of what is
> does not open the door directly
> to what *should be*.
> . . . the ultimate goal itself
> and the longing to reach it
> must come from another source.
>
> . . . religion is the age-old endeavor of mankind
> to become clearly and completely conscious
> of these values and goals
> and constantly to
> strengthen and extend their effect.
> If one conceives of religion and science
> according to these definitions
> then a conflict between them appears impossible.
> . . . nevertheless there exist between the two
> strong reciprocal relationships . . .
> The situation may be expressed by an image:
> science without religion is lame,
> religion without science is blind."

Several approaches have evolved - to incorporate modern views in traditional faiths. In reform churches and temples, teachings from holy books may focus on symbolic truths, and downplay the supernatural and miracles. And, in more traditional congregations, individuals may have their own non-literal ways of viewing Biblical stories, and the words they say when they join with others in prayer.

These approaches work well for many people. By adapting ancient traditions to accommodate modern views, a body of ancient wisdom is retained. And, people also retain the community and the rituals and celebrations that, for many, are the main attraction in religion.

## A choice

But, for many, this compromise is unsatisfying, and it avoids confronting a core issue. For, a world view defines what we think is possible, and this can shape how we decide what to do. An example of this is seen in a joke:

> Heavy rains flooded a town. A rescue boat arrived, but one man refused to get in. "God will save me," he said. "Rescue others whose need is greater."
>
> The water rose higher, and the boat returned. The man refused again. And he refused a third time, when a helicopter came as he was clinging to his roof.
>
> The man drowned that night. And, in heaven, he had a question.
>
> He said, "God, you know I've always believed in you and I have lived a righteous life. Why didn't you save me from the flood?"
>
> God replied, "I sent two boats and a helicopter. What else did you want?"

A related example - clearly, not a joke - can be seen in suicide bombers. If this is seen as an act that will be rewarded with eternal bliss, it can be logical, or even desirable - a worthwhile deal - to forfeit one's life on earth.

The issue comes down to a "yes or no" question.

Is there a force or a being – God - who hears individual prayers and may cause a miracle to determine a specific event?

For example, if a child is near death from a disease with no known cure, might a divine act - prompted by prayers or God's unprompted intervention - remove the disease and restore the child to health?

Or, if a well-aimed bullet is shot at close range - could a supernatural guardian prevent it from entering the body?

## Yes, or no?

If the answer is yes, then what follows is a view in which our fate, and the fate of the world, is in God's hands.

A hurricane destroys a village. A war rages and thousands are killed. In a contest, one is champion while others lose. By actively shaping events, or by declining to act - each of these occurred as God intended. Each was part of God's plan.

With this as the way of the world, we have a relationship with God. We worship and try to follow His laws. We pray - for strength and guidance - and we may ask for specific things for ourselves and our loved ones. We work to reach our goals, and we hope to be blessed with good fortune.

Millions see the world this way. Western culture has had this view for centuries. But this is not compatible with a science-based understanding of what seems possible.

If the answer is no, then what follows is a world that operates within the bounds of natural laws.

So, when a hurricane or a war causes destruction, these are seen as forces of nature and decisions of men. And, in a game, if a ball bounces just inside of the line - it did this solely because of speed and spin and wind and other forces. No guiding hand had a role.

In this view, our fate is based, in part, on our actions and, in part, by forces that are beyond our control. Elements of chance and randomness exist. And, when "miracles" occur, they are signs of a long-shot beating the odds (as in heads being flipped 10 times in a row) or that the experts were wrong in their predictions.

Yes or no?

We can't have it both ways. And, there is no honest middle ground.

These options are similar to those described in a quote from Joseph Campbell.

> "One is 'the way of the kitten'; the other, 'the way of the monkey'.
> When a kitten cries 'Miaow', its mother, coming, takes it by the scruff and carries it to safety; but as anyone who has ever traveled in India will have observed, when a band of monkeys come scampering down from a tree and across the road, the babies riding on their mothers' backs are hanging on by themselves. Accordingly, with reference to the two attitudes:
>> the first is that of the person who prays, 'O Lord, O Lord, come save me!' and
>> the second of one who, without such prayers or cries, goes to work on himself.
>
> In Japan the same two are known as *tariki*, 'outside strength', or 'power from without', and *jiriki*, 'own strength', 'effort or power from within'".

## Ways of belief - with no miracles

Many do, however, hold views of God that do not conflict with science. These recognize a force of creation, an ordering principle, or a spirit in all things. But they do not believe in a God that intervenes in human events.

Some prominent views are described below. Each contains an element of how Einstein saw the world.

Differences in these are due, in part, to shades of emphasis. And, in part, they may be due to semantics. For, what some call "God" is similar, in many ways, to what others see as "forces of Nature". (For example, the God referred to by Einstein is very different from the God in the Bible.)

Deism

This view includes belief in a supreme being. But, it views this as a God who created the universe, then left it to move forward on its own. It feels that God has no involvement in human affairs and does not control or influence natural events.

This view has been popular in several eras, including the 1700s. Many of America's founding fathers, including George Washington, Ben Franklin, and Thomas Jefferson, are said to have held this view. The following quote from Albert Einstein has also been described as consistent with Deism:

> "My religion consists of a humble admiration of the illimitable superior spirit who reveals himself in the slight details we are able to perceive with our frail and feeble minds. That deeply emotional conviction of the presence of a superior reasoning power, which is revealed in the incomprehensible universe, forms my idea of God."

Deism acknowledges the obvious fact that our universe was, somehow, created, and that the wondrous diversity and beauty of life prompts respect for the order that underlies it. With the exception of the imagined qualities it assigns to the creator (with an assumption of some type of mind or will in a deity), this is similar to Einstein's view.

Pantheism

Pantheism is the belief that God is identical with the whole natural world; that everything is God. Unlike the traditional Western view, where God is one type of presence, and all creatures are separate, pantheism sees God *as* the universe; all things in our world are part of God, and nothing is separate or distinct from God. And, thus, each person, and each raindrop and flower, is part of God.

This is similar to views of Baruch Spinoza (1632-1677), who felt that "God" and "Nature" were two names for the same reality; the force that pervades and gives order to the universe and of which all substances, all creatures, and all people are manifestations.

Einstein related to this view, also, as is shown in his statement:

"I believe In Spinoza's God, who reveals Himself in the orderly harmony of what exists, not in a God who concerns himself with fates and actions of human beings."

Secular Humanism

This approach has been defined as "a rational philosophy informed by science, inspired by art, and motivated by compassion." It sees the natural world as all that is, and rejects the concepts of God and the supernatural. It affirms our ability to lead meaningful, ethical lives, without need for a deity, and it advocates using reason to work toward a more humane society.

Albert Einstein joined the American Humanist Association in the 1950s.

Atheism

Atheists believe that there is no God. Here, the focus is on what they do not believe. This group has no consistent view on what *is* believed.

Some who describe themselves as atheists are not at all spiritual. However, some others, while rejecting the traditional definition of God, may have an appreciation for the beauty and order in our world that is not very different from some who describe themselves as believers.

Einstein was seen by some as an atheist, because of his lack of belief in a personal God. Einstein acknowledged this. But, as is shown in statements he made in two letters, he preferred to avoid the connotation of this term:

> "From the viewpoint of a Jesuit priest I am, of course, and have always been an atheist."

> "I have repeatedly said that in my opinion the idea of a personal God is a childlike one. You may call me an agnostic, but I do not share the crusading spirit of the professional atheist whose fervor is mostly due to a painful act of liberation from the fetters of religious indoctrination received in youth. I prefer an attitude of humility corresponding to the weakness of our intellectual understanding of nature and of our own being."

As shown above, Einstein's spiritual views are not able to be given simple labels. They are broader than available categories. And, by including perspectives from modern physics and cosmology, they contain an element of something new.

## Tao

One additional view should be examined - the ancient Chinese perspective of Tao (which is translated, in English, as "the Way").

This has some important parallels to Einstein's views. It recognizes a creative force - a spirit that is present in all things, and that we can look to, learn from, and relate to. It sees order in the universe, and nature as a way to discover that order. But it has no view of a God who may intervene in events.

This is not to suggest that Einstein thought of himself as Taoist. But, for those who may be skeptical that Einstein's type of spirituality is something untested and new, it can be useful to see that it is similar, in some ways, to a widely-accepted view that is very old.

This can be seen in the following quotes from Taoist texts.

There was something formless and perfect
before the universe was born.
It is serene. Empty.
Solitary. Unchanging.
Infinite. Eternally present.
It is the mother of the universe.
For lack of a better name,
I call it the Tao.


Mountains are high because of it,
oceans are deep because of it,
animals run because of it,
birds fly because of it.

The Tao gives birth to all beings, . . .
creating without possessing,
acting without expecting,
guiding without interfering.


Every being in the universe
is an expression of the Tao.

The Way is the basis of virtue,
the root of heaven,
the door of fortune.
All beings depend on it
for life, growth, and stability. . .
there is nothing it does not do;
no one knows its state,
no one knows its reality,
but there is truth in it.


It flows through all things,
inside and outside, and returns
to the origin of all things.

Thus the Way effects
the movement of the heavens
and the stability of the earth,
turning endlessly like a wheel,
flowing ceaselessly like water.
It is there at the beginning and end of things:
as wind rises, clouds condense,
thunder rumbles, and rain falls,
it responds in concert infinitely.


. . . it harmonizes dark and light,
regulates the four seasons,
and tunes the forces of nature.


The Tao is called the Great Mother:
empty yet inexhaustible,
it gives birth to infinite worlds.
It is always present within you.

The Tao gives rise to all forms,
yet it has no form of its own.
If you attempt to fix a picture of it in your mind,
you will lose it.


The Tao never does anything,
yet through it all things are done.


Form that includes all forms,
image without an image,
subtle, beyond all conception.


It is hidden but always present.
I don't know who gave birth to it.
It is older than God.

How can the divine Oneness be seen?
In beautiful forms, breathtaking wonders,
awe-inspiring miracles?
The Tao is not obliged to present itself this way.
It is always present and always available.
When speech is exhausted and mind dissolved,
it presents itself.
When clarity and purity are cultivated,
it reveals itself.
When sincerity is unconditional,
it unveils itself.
If you are willing to be lived by it,
you will see it everywhere,
even in the most ordinary things.

You can't know it, but you can be it,
at ease in your own life.
Just realize where you come from:
this is the essence of wisdom.


Man follows the earth.
Earth follows the universe.
The universe follows the Tao.
The Tao follows only itself.

# New Kind of Faith

> "Try and penetrate with our limited means the secrets of nature and you will find that, behind all the discernible concatenations, there remains something subtle, intangible, and inexplicable. Veneration for this force beyond anything that we can comprehend is my religion."
>
> Albert Einstein

An ancient Hindu text begins with a scene on a battlefield at dawn. A great struggle is about to begin, and Prince Arjuna is tormented with conflicting views of what is right, and what he should do. He is overcome with sadness and despair.

This is a metaphor for struggles we all face - in major challenges and decisions, and in everyday tests or "moments of truth". We may be uncertain, confused, or afraid and we wish for help.

These types of feelings sparked the saying, "There are no atheists in foxholes."

But, if we don't believe in a heavenly father, we are on our own. And, apart from the support we may receive from family and friends, we must, ourselves, summon the strength we need to get through difficult times.

This is not as comforting as a sense of personal connection with a God who guides events and loves us. And, when facing death, it's hard to beat the prospect of heaven.

But, regardless of belief, approaches that are used in challenging times are very similar.

> When searching for wisdom or strength,
>    people meditate and pray.
>
> And, when faced with hardship or sorrow,
>    we apply our faith.

These are age-old parts of religious practices. And, when examined with the methods of science, their benefits have been confirmed. But, it has also been shown that these benefits are not dependent on the supernatural.

## Meditation and prayer

Prayer, for the most part, is directed to a personal god. But, those with different views may also pray.

One part of this is a way of expressing hope.

"Please, let this be good news."

"Please, let her be cured from disease."

Or, "Let me let me get this job," or find a parking space, or any number of trivial or important things.

Often, there is no thought that "anyone" is listening as we beseech the powers that be. We simply have a wish and think these thoughts, and may say these words out loud.

But some, more intentionally, direct their thoughts out toward the unseen power (however they understand it) that causes things to be as they will be.

And, like a reflection or an echo,

they may feel that something bounces back -

that sheds light on a question

or conveys new meaning

or confirms what they've suspected all along.

By asking, they receive.

They hear with different ears, and see with different eyes -

better able to appreciate and understand.

Prayer can be a quiet time - to gather thoughts, and to give thanks or show respect or appreciation. And, as we articulate questions, concerns, or desires, we may touch deep levels of understanding. For while prayer, in an overt way, is directed out toward a god or infinite presence, the main value, for many, is as a way of reaching within.

Theologians and surveys reinforce this. For example, a Gallup survey found that the majority who claimed a personal relationship with God said they gained "strength to deal with problems", rather than direct intervention in their lives. Rabbi Kushner had a similar view, as he described prayer as a way to "tap hidden reserves of faith and courage", and something that may offer social and other benefits.

> " . . . you didn't get a miracle to avert a tragedy. But you discovered people around you, and God beside you, and strength within you to help you survive the tragedy. I offer that as an example of a prayer being answered."

In other words,
> "Prayer does not change God,
> but it changes him who prays."

Medical research has shown that prayer can offer an increased sense of well-being. It may also reduce anxiety, promote a more positive outlook, and offer a sense of calm.

Meditation has similar benefits. Studies have shown that it is clearly relaxing. Heart rate and breathing slow. Brain waves change. It can bring a sense of calm, and focus the mind.

As Dr. Herbert Benson described this, meditation (and related techniques) . . .

> " . . . quiet the mind and the body to a more substantial degree and with greater speed than any other means. We know that the experience seems to clean the slate of the mind, making it more receptive and creative. And we know that the experience feels very spiritual to some people, and that spirituality agrees with them . . ."

Regardless of what one believes, these sources of strength and wisdom are available.

> In looking out –
> we ponder the forces that determine what is,
> and seek to find a path we should take.

> By looking within –
> we become open to deeper layers of our minds,
> to ways of knowing that we otherwise could not reach.

As we meditate or pray, we get a state of mind that may offer distinctive insights and perspectives. We may feel a relaxing calm. And we may gain a sense of acceptance and peace.

## Faith

Separate from having techniques available to calm ourselves and prepare, we may take a view of trust and acceptance.

Recognizing that much of what occurs is beyond our control,

> we can have hope – that things may go as we desire, or work out for the best.

> And we may try to gain the peace that comes with feeling that, whatever occurs, all of what we see makes sense (in a way), and all is as it is meant to be . . .

Faith has been defined, in part, as "a trusting acceptance of God's will". For those who understand "God's will" as the expression of natural laws, acceptance can begin with observing.

> By studying nature, we can get a sense of what is, and principles that lie behind what we see.

> By studying history, we can observe what people have done, and get a sense of what we seem inclined to do.

> If these are the ways of the world and the types of things that occur, then, these can be seen as expressions of "God's will".

This shows a world with clear patterns and order. But, it does not show a world that was designed to grant our wishes.

We see death and disease, natural disasters and wars, aggression, and injustice - a world where chance events can be tragic. But we also see kindness, beauty, and love.

We see attempts at justice and some common ideals that have been shared in different cultures and times. We see visions that point toward a better world and ways to be better people, and we see steps in which individuals and cultures have tried to move themselves toward this.

This tendency - to sense and strive toward ideals - is something we can have faith in.

Einstein referred to this, as he pointed to " . . . the Good, the True, and the Beautiful in humanity", and said

"I believe in the brotherhood of man . . ."

And, for some, this sense - of all that is right and good - is, in itself, how they understand their God.

> Here, God is a symbol of all that is good and wise,
> and not an actual supernatural presence.

As in the traditional view, this symbol - God - is magnificent and pure, with a power that prompts action and devotion. It represents our highest ideals - what people are inspired by and strive toward. And, while it is invisible, untouchable, intangible - this presence is something that both our hearts and our minds can know is true.

The ugly and evil and tragic and unfair have always been present, along with the good. Both, therefore, seem to be part of God's plan. We may not understand or be pleased by what occurs. But, with an attitude of faith, we can accept it - and, thereby find the kind of peace that comes with not resenting or being disillusioned or confused.

This has parallels to the faith that many place in a personal God. For, while a science-based view may not imagine that all is directed by a presence that cares for each individual, it can have faith that, as all things act in accordance with their natures, there are reasons why things occur as they do, and all that happens makes sense as part of a larger plan.

Whatever form it takes - having faith seems, clearly, to offer benefits. Medical studies have shown that those who described themselves as believers had better health outcomes than those who did not. They were more optimistic, with less depression, anxiety, hostility, and substance abuse.

Faith can help people make peace with hardship or illness. As some have put it, they:

> "took control over what I could and gave the rest up to God."

Also, it just feels good - to be hopeful and at ease.

The exact nature of belief doesn't seem to matter.

> "I can say that, according to my investigations, it does not matter which God you worship, nor which theology you adopt as your own. Spiritual life, in general, is very healthy."
> Dr. Herbert Benson

In the book, *"Who Needs God?"*, Rabbi Kushner wrote:

> "You become a certain kind of person when you choose to believe there is a pattern and purpose to the universe, when you learn to see the world through the eyes of faith."

For those who cannot believe in a personal god, faith can be based in Einstein's God.

# A New Kind of Religion

> "A religion . . . that stressed the magnificence of the universe as revealed by modern science, might be able to draw forth reserves of reverence and awe hardly tapped by the conventional faiths. Sooner or later, such a religion will emerge."
>
> Carl Sagan

Since the time of Copernicus, then accelerating with Darwin and continuing in modern times, insights from science have affected religion.

One outcome has been changes in traditional faiths.

Another is that spiritual views that are consistent with science may be laying the groundwork for something new.

These point toward different options in the "new kind of religion" Einstein described.

## Incorporating modern views in traditional faiths

Religions have had to confront the fact that a number of traditional views do not fit with how we now understand the world.

Some reform churches and temples have reinterpreted ancient teachings, to align with modern views. Images of God are symbolic or vague, biblical stories are valued as myth, and messages focus on personal and social issues.

This approach enables many who have a modern world view to continue to practice traditional religions. But, a backlash has also occurred. Some with Orthodox views feel these approaches have strayed so far from core beliefs that they are no longer the same religions. And, in classrooms and courtrooms and public debates, fundamentalists have challenged findings from science that conflict with what is written in the Bible.

But, even with modern adaptations, many remain unsatisfied with traditional religion. They may disagree with core messages, or find it hard to suspend disbelief. Or, when surrounded by believers who see things more literally, they may feel uncomfortable viewing teachings in symbolic terms.

As they consider plusses and minuses, the question - another choice - may arise.

> Is it better to:
>> continue with an ancient structure, with modern patches and adjustments;
>>> or
>> to keep good things that are recognized from the past, but build with these on a new foundation?

## Forming something new

No significant groups have formed, with a focus on Einstein's views. But, in books and journals and in conferences and classrooms, the relationship between science and religion is being examined.

With a sense of reverence and perspectives from sociobiology and physics, Carl Sagan, EO Wilson, Fritjof Capra, and many others have described new ways of seeing ourselves and our world. A new vision is emerging, with new ways of looking at age-old questions:

> Who are we?
>
> How did this all come to be?
>
> And, based on our understanding of our nature and our world - what, then, should we do?

Since they were first published in the 1920s, Einstein's views have been part of this discussion. With elements of deism and pantheism, and with a flavor consistent with Tao, these express reverence for the unseen force that shapes our world. They recognize the importance of intuition and emotion. But, they also require that, rather than just accepting things on faith, views fit with a rational understanding.

Some find this perspective interesting and, as they examine spiritual approaches, they may include ideas from this as part of their personal views. Some others may feel a stronger connection - to the point that the spiritual perspective Einstein described fits as well with their own gut feeling as anything they have seen. If asked what they believe (and, without a better way to describe it), they could say they believe in Einstein's God.

## Spiritual practice (vs. beliefs)

It can be useful to have a clear sense of what one does, and does not believe, and to have simple way of describing one's sense of religion. This sense of focus or definition may all that a number of people need.

But, this falls short of what some have described as a defining quality of religion - in having an <u>active</u> relationship with the unseen power (however one understands it) that underlies all that is. Without active involvement, views are more "philosophy" than "religion" - and they may lack the power to satisfy on deep emotional levels that can be found in traditional faiths. In the spirit that Catholics take communion and Jews keep kosher, rituals bring beliefs to life and turn ideas into things we physically experience.

Informally, and often with no sense of doing things on these terms, many who feel secular in their orientation (or, in accord with Einstein's views) engage in spiritual activities.

For example, for Einstein, seeking knowledge was an expression of faith. He said:

> "I am of the opinion that all the finer speculations in the realm of science spring from a deep religious feeling . . . I also believe that this kind of religiousness . . . is the only creative religious activity of our time."

Few people are scientists, but many feel an urge to learn more about how things work, and why things are the way they are. In the spirit of "seek, and you shall find",

> some study nature, or human nature;
>
> some explore philosophy, history, or world religions.

And, beyond the satisfaction that may come as they increase their understanding, they may feel a connection with the mysteries that lie at the core of what they are exploring.

Seeking knowledge was a path that suited Einstein. But, a wide range of activities may offer ways of spiritual practice for different people.

Some commune with nature.

> They heed the words of John Muir -
>
>> "Climb the mountains and get their good tidings. Nature's peace will flow into you as sunshine flows into trees."
>
> "all the world seems a church and the mountains altars."

In walks - on the beach, or in the woods and fields - they listen and observe. And, as they examine buds on trees, or look to the stars at night, or have relationships with animals, they may feel a sense of connection . . .

Some perform ritual acts.

In the spirit of ancient dietary laws, some avoid meat or veal or certain fishes or other foods.

And, in the spirit of ancient offerings, some use candles or water, or make gestures of appreciation, or act in particular ways that seem in keeping with the spirit of an unseen power.

Some express their faith through actions (good works).

By helping those in need, they may feel they are acting in a spirit that seems in line with the best aspects of our nature.

Some take efforts to protect the environment, or to preserve and maintain open spaces.

Some are "religious" in their commitment to recycling, use of energy-efficient vehicles, and other aspects of conservation. Separate from the impact these activities may have on the environment, they are statements of belief and ways of putting values into practice.

Some meditate or pray.

Some go on journeys to sacred places.

Some dance or sing or paint or compose.

With no church or set rituals, the spiritual practices of those who share Einstein's view are mainly individual.

But, as Earth Day is celebrated, in concerts by spiritual artists, in demonstrations against injustice and other events, people gather in groups and feel the power that comes with communal purpose and shared feeling.

And, at weddings, funerals, and other occasions that mark life events, the words that are spoken and songs that are sung now often focus on themes of love and commitment, the inevitability of change, and other things that are universal and eternal - rather than on a deity watching over.

The specific actions each person is drawn to vary, just as personalities vary and inclinations can vary - based on age, culture, moment in history, etc. But, all are ways of connecting with something larger, or efforts to act in accordance with ideals.

Certain types of experiences can give a spiritual mind-set. And, in some cases, they can bring a sense of connection - to the force or spirit or presence (however one understands it) that is contained in all of nature, and all that is.

The sense of what one is connecting to may be vague. But, consistent with Einstein's descriptions (and, consistent with Tao), this is not seen as a problem or failure, but as an accurate reflection of what is, and is not, understood.

Rather than attaching assumed and human-like qualities to the powers that be, Einstein's perspective clearly recognizes that some type of force (embedded in natural laws) underlies all we see, but it acknowledges that the nature of this remains unclear, and may perhaps forever be unknowable.

But, while this force is vague, it is somehow familiar. It is part of us. It is what makes us aware and alive. And, if we step away from daily busyness, and if we choose to open ourselves, we may feel a sense of its presence.

## A middle ground

Being oriented toward Einstein's God does not require rejecting the old. In fact, the opposite is the case, where much in traditional wisdom can be revered.

The main changes that have come with a modern world view are in our understanding of the material world. But, these do not affect the complex realms of ethics and laws, ways to forgiveness, or how to live well with one another. Here, we need insights that draw from the best of what we know - from religion, along with literature, history, philosophy, and other realms.

With respect for ways the divine has long been understood and worshipped, those who reject the supernatural may remain "cultural adherents" - holding modern beliefs, but continuing to appreciate ancient writings and observing some ancient traditions. We may no longer view these as literal, as things that actually happened as written. But, when viewed in a symbolic sense or as myth - we can view these (like the music of Mozart) as "divinely inspired" - in recognizing the genius of authors to touch on something true, and strike a chord that people have responded to for centuries.

With this, we may be inspired by stories of freedom and forgiveness. We can see how the symbol of a personal god can offer a connection with the divine. We can see a covenant with God as a commitment to ideals. And we can see Jesus as child of God, and how following the goodness he embodied can be a path to salvation.

Much as Greek myths remain valuable, long after the religion they were based in declined, images and stories from a range of traditions can help us consider issues in our lives.

We may be drawn to cathedrals, and moved by religious music and art. And, to gain the emotional power of marking life events as our ancestors have for centuries, we may get married in a church or under a chuppah, or observe traditional rites for funerals and births. We may celebrate traditional holidays. And, as we can observe Halloween without identifying ourselves as pagans, we may observe Christmas and Easter, or Passover and Rosh Hashanah - as cultural or family traditions - without needing to be active members of these religions.

This has parallels with the past. When Christianity replaced pagan belief, many elements of older traditions were retained. And, just as the meaning of Easter is enhanced by elements from the pagan rites of spring, future celebrations may draw from enduring elements of what has come before. Much as a tree adds new rings but retains its core as it grows, many traditional views will remain when something new is formed.

## One among many

An ancient story - an analogy for religion - tells of blind men who were asked to describe an elephant.

> One touched the trunk, and said the elephant was like a snake.
>
> One touched the tusk, and said the elephant was like a spear.
>
> A third touched the belly, and described the elephant as a wall.
>
> Another touched the ear, and said the elephant was like a piece of cloth.

Given limits in what we can see, and different perspectives, there will be different views of the divine.

And, just as the elephant remains an elephant, regardless of how blind men perceive it; the force that directs our world is what it is, separate from what we think we understand.

With many views of the divine, there are many religions, and many paths to God. And, as Einstein's sense of God becomes more widely understood, this view may be acknowledged as a type of belief.

This approach is not for everyone. But, for those who have a sense of something spiritual but reject the supernatural, it can offer a way to affirm belief in something positive. Rather than accepting a label - as atheist, agnostic, or "none/other" - that is based in what is not believed, they can affirm what they do believe.

## A path to the future

As Einstein's view becomes more widely understood, people may meet and talk. Ideas may expand. Books may be assembled - to communicate shared beliefs and offer collections of parables, sermons, myths, and prayers - with images and insights that reflect a spiritual sense that does not include a personal God. These, with music, ritual, and art, may offer a focus for worship and study. Groups may be formed, and leaders may emerge. And, if they are presented in ways people are drawn to and accept, these views could form a core of a new religion.

Or, these views may remain a more private affair.

For, some feel that religion requires the supernatural. And without the promise of miracles or everlasting life (or without the threat of damnation), these views may not provide the incentive or spark that moves people to declare their faith, and to gather with others in worship.

Whatever form it takes, and whether it becomes prominent or not, Einstein's God provides a foundation for a type of belief that fits with a modern understanding. As a voice in what may be a type of emerging Western Tao, it points to a Way - of being spiritual without the supernatural.

# Postscript

**From New York Times Magazine**
November 9, 1930

With primitive man it is above all fear that evokes religious notions - fear of hunger, wild beasts, sickness, death. Since at this stage of existence understanding of causal connections is usually poorly developed, the human mind creates illusory beings more or less analogous to itself on whose wills and actions these fearful happenings depend. Thus one tries to secure the favor of these beings by carrying out actions and offering sacrifices which, according to the tradition handed down from generation to generation, propitiate them or make them well disposed toward a mortal. In this sense I am speaking of a religion of fear...

The social impulses are another source of the crystallization of religion. Fathers and mothers and the leaders of larger human communities are mortal and fallible. The desire for guidance, love, and support prompts men to form the social or moral conception of God. This is the God of Providence, who protects, disposes, rewards, and punishes; the God who, according to the limits of the believer's outlook, loves and cherishes the life of the tribe or of the human race, or even or life itself; the comforter in sorrow and unsatisfied longing; he who preserves the souls of the dead. This is the social or moral conception of God.

The Jewish scriptures admirably illustrate the development from the religion of fear to moral religion, a development continued in the New Testament. The religions of all civilized peoples, especially the peoples of the Orient, are primarily moral religions.

... there is a third stage of religious experience ... I shall call it cosmic religious feeling. It is very difficult to elucidate this feeling to anyone who is entirely without it, especially as there is no anthropomorphic conception of God corresponding to it. The individual feels the futility of human desires and aims and the sublimity and marvelous order which reveal themselves both in nature and in the world of thought. Individual existence impresses him as a sort of prison and he wants to experience the universe as a single significant whole. . .

The religious geniuses of all ages have been distinguished by this kind of religious feeling, which knows no dogma and no God conceived in man's image; so that there can be no church whose central teachings are based on it. Hence it is precisely among the heretics of every age that we find men who were filled with this highest kind of religious feeling and were in many cases regarded by their contemporaries as atheists, sometimes also as saints. Looked at in this light, men like Democritus, Francis of Assisi, and Spinoza are closely akin to one another.

How can cosmic religious feeling be communicated from one person to another, if it can give rise to no definite notion of a God and no theology? In my view, it is the most important function of art and science to awaken this feeling and keep it alive in those who are receptive to it.

Albert Einstein

# Notes

This section identifies sources for quotes used in this book. It also provides some additional descriptions and quotes, to clarify aspects of Einstein's spiritual views. Sources of Einstein's quotes are identified base on the date and setting in which his statements were published, spoken, or recorded. Many of these have been reprinted in multiple publications, and the collections assembled and edited by Alice Calaprice and books by Helen Dukas and others have been used to identify or confirm original sources.

## Preface

**Millions, around the world, share this view**
Many surveys have shown that substantial percentages of people in North America and Europe have a spiritual sense that differs from traditional religions. For example, a 2006 survey reported that 36% of respondents in the UK held humanist, rather than religious views on the basis for our sense of right and wrong, the potential for an afterlife, and other topics. In the United States, a Gallup poll reported that 30% described themselves as "spiritual but not religious".
British Humanist Association website
G. Gallup. Public Perspective, May/June 2000, p. 15
**deeply religious nonbeliever**
Albert Einstein. Letter to Hans Muehsam, March, 1954
(Calaprice, p. 218)

## Introduction

**Einstein was a giant**
Richard Feynman, beginning a lecture; Meade, p. 26

## Einstein's God

*(All quotes in this chapter are from Albert Einstein)*

**I am a deeply religious nonbeliever**
    Letter to Hans Muehsam, March, 1954
       (Calaprice, p. 218)
**I cannot conceive of a personal God**
    Letter to a banker, August, 1927 (Dukas, p. 66)
**There is nothing divine about morality**
    The World As I See It, p. 29
**I do not believe in immortality**
    1953, Einstein archive (Calaprice, p. 217)
**Mere unbelief in a personal God is no philosophy at all**
    Letter to V. T. Aaltonen, May, 1952 (Calaprice, p. 216)
**Everyone who is seriously involved in the pursuit of science**
    Letter to Phyllis Wright, January, 1936 (Calaprice, p. 211)
**You will hardly find one among ... scientific minds**
    The World As I See It, p. 28-29
**It is ... a feeling of awe**
    Letter to a rabbi, December, 1939 (Dukas, p.69-70)
**If something is in me which can be called religious**
    From a letter, March, 1954 (Dukas, p. 43)
**I cannot conceive of a God who rewards and punishes**
    The World As I See It, p. 5
**My religion consists of a humble admiration**
    From a letter, 1927 (Dukas, p. 66)
**I believe in Spinoza's God**
    Telegram to a Jewish newspaper, 1929 (Calaprice, p. 204)
**I believe in the brotherhood of man**
    Clark, p. 724
**The fairest thing we can experience is the mysterious**
    The World as I See It, p. 5

## The Way of Science

**The further the spiritual evolution of mankind advances**
    Albert Einstein. Science, Philosophy, and Religion:
    A Symposium, 1941 (Ideas and Opinions, p. 53)

**He had an emotional response**
Emotion was a critical part of Einstein's sense of religion. In quotes in the previous chapter, he spoke of "rapturous amazement", "a feeling of awe", "humble admiration", and a sense of "wonder". He described his idea of God as "That deeply emotional conviction of the presence of a superior reasoning power . . ."
**We are in the position of a little child entering a huge library**
Albert Einstein. Interview with George Viereck, 1929
(Brian, p. 186)
In a similar statement, Einstein said:
We know nothing about it [God, the world] at all. All our knowledge is but the knowledge of school-children. Possibly we shall know a little more than we do now. But the real nature of things, that we shall never know, never.
Albert Einstein. Interview- the Jewish Sentinel, 1931
(Calaprice, p. 207)
**nature as an expression of the force that guides our world**
My comprehension of God comes from the deeply felt conviction of a superior intelligence that reveals itself in the knowable world.
Albert Einstein. An answer to a question, 1923
(Calaprice, p. 203)
The divine reveals itself in the physical world.
Albert Einstein. Rosenkranz, p. 88
**as we begin to understand . . . we may get a glimpse –**
**into the force that causes all things to be as they are**
Nature is showing us only the tail of the lion, but I have no doubt that the lion belongs to it even though, because of its large size, it cannot totally reveal itself at once. We can see it only the way a louse that is sitting on it would.
Albert Einstein. To Heinrich Zangger, 1914
(Calaprice, p. 232)
Look deep, deep into nature, and then you will understand everything better.
Albert Einstein. To Margot Einstein, 1951
(Calaprice, p. 62)

**the attempt to understand expresses a type of reverence**

While it is true that scientific results are entirely independent of religious or moral considerations, those individuals to whom we owe the great creative achievements in science were all imbued with the truly religious conviction that this universe of ours is something perfect and is responsive to the rational striving for knowledge.

    Albert Einstein. Response to the Liberal Minister's Club, 1948; Ideas and Opinions, p. 56

In every true searcher of Nature, there is a kind of religious reverence.

    Albert Einstein. 1920 (Calaprice, p. 202)

A contemporary has said, not unjustly, that in this materialistic age of ours the serious scientific workers are the only profoundly religious people.

    Albert Einstein. The World as I See It, p. 28

**the goal and method of science - "striving after rational knowledge" - could be a Way of spiritual practice and seeking**

I cannot conceive of a God who rewards and punishes his creatures, or has a will of the type of which we are conscious in ourselves. An individual who should survive his physical death is also beyond my comprehension, nor do I wish it otherwise . . . Enough for me the mystery of the eternity of life, and the inkling of the marvelous structure of reality, together with the single-hearted endeavor to comprehend a portion, be it never so tiny, of the reason that manifests itself in nature.

    Albert Einstein. The World as I See It, p. 5

. . . whoever has undergone the intense experience of successful advances made in this domain [science], is moved by the profound reverence for the rationality made manifest in existence. By way of the understanding he achieves a far reaching emancipation from the shackles of personal hopes and desires, and thereby attains that humble attitude of mind toward the grandeur of reason, incarnate in existence, and which, in its profoundest depths, is inaccessible to man. This attitude, however, appears to me to be religious in the highest sense of the word. And so it seems to me that science not only purifies the religious impulse of the dross of its anthropomorphism but also contributes to a religious spiritualization of our understanding of life.

    Albert Einstein. Science, Philosophy, and Religion: A Symposium, 1941 (Ideas and Opinions, p. 52-3)

Strenuous intellectual work and the study of God's Nature are the angels that will lead me through all the troubles of this life

    Albert Einstein. To Pauline Winteler, 1897 (Calaprice, p. 5)
I want to know how God created this world. I am not interested in this or that phenomenon... I want to know his thoughts.

    Albert Einstein. To a student, 1920
    (Calaprice, p. 202)

**striving after rational knowledge**

    Albert Einstein. Science, Philosophy, and Religion: A Symposium, 1941 (Ideas and Opinions, p. 53)

**When a view holds up - we accept it**

This approach = the scientific method

The Dali Lama has said that, if science were to show that his beliefs were not accurate, he would change his beliefs.

    Newberg, Why We Believe What We Believe, p. 213

**Eastern views, which see knowledge as a path to enlightenment**

In the Hindu tradition, jnana yoga is a path of knowledge. In the Buddhist tradition, first item in 8-fold path is "right view" (or "right understanding").

**basing beliefs on ancient revelations, as written in holy books**

A scientific person will never understand why he should believe opinions only because they are written in a certain book. [Furthermore], he will never believe that the results of his own attempts are final.

    Albert Einstein. To J. Lee, 1945
    (Calaprice, p. 254)

**maintaining belief - when evidence suggests it may be false**

As Mark Twain put this,

"Faith is believing what you know ain't so."

    Pudd'nhead Wilson

**Einstein considered but could not accept many concepts in traditional religion**

Thus I came . . . to a deep religiosity, which, however, reached an abrupt end at the age of twelve. Through the reading of popular scientific books I soon reached a conviction that much in the stories of the Bible could not be true . . . Suspicion against every kind of authority grew out of this experience . . . an attitude that has never left me.

    Albert Einstein. Autobiographical notes, p. 3

**He recognized the appeal of these**
> Nobody, certainly, will deny that the idea of the existence of an omnipotent, just, and omnibeneficent personal God is able to accord man solace, help, and guidance . . .
>> Albert Einstein. Ideas and Opinions, p. 50

**He knew it was not possible to disprove them**
> To be sure, the doctrine of a personal God interfering with natural events could never be *refuted,* in the real sense, by science, for this doctrine can always take refuge in those domains in which scientific knowledge has not yet been able to set foot.
>> Albert Einstein. Ideas and Opinions, p. 51

**He saw the world as wholly based in natural laws**
> In the beginning (if there was such a thing), God created Newton's laws of motion together with the necessary masses and forces. That is all . . . all events, including the actions of mankind, are determined by laws of nature.
>> Albert Einstein. Autobiographical Notes, p. 17

**this, also, could not be proven . . . it served as a type of belief**
> . . . it must be admitted that our actual knowledge of these laws is only imperfect and fragmentary, so that, actually, the belief in the existence of basic all-embracing laws in Nature also rests on a sort of faith. All the same this faith has been largely justified so far by the success of scientific research.
>> Albert Einstein – letter to a child, 1936 (Dukas, p. 32-3)

> I have no better expression than 'religious' for this confidence in the rational nature of reality . . .
>> Albert Einstein – to Maurine Solovine, January, 1951 (Calaprice, p. 216)

**I don't try to imagine a God**
>> Albert Einstein. Letter to S. Flesch, 1954 (Calaprice p. 219)

**A rational view is not the only way of understanding**
As was explained in an earlier Note in this chapter, Einstein recognized emotion as an important aspect of understanding. And, as a scientist with boldly original ideas, he recognized the importance of intuition and inspiration.

> I believe in intuition and inspiration . . . At times I feel certain I am right while not knowing the reason.
>> Albert Einstein. 1931. (Calaprice p. 287)

> It is better for people to be like the beasts . . . they should be more intuitive; they should not be too conscious of what they are doing while they are doing it.
>> Albert Einstein. 1940. (Calaprice, p. 119)

His religiousness was related to a sense "that behind anything that can be experienced there is a something that our mind cannot grasp".
Albert Einstein. My Credo, 1932

**The Way of Science plays a critical role in values**
Apart from the view of many believers, that values are given by God and expressed through religion (and the view, by CS Lewis and others, that the presence of ethical behavior compels belief in God as the source of this goodness), rational analysis - in evaluating what works and what seems best - has long been an essential element in our sense of right and wrong. This is used in the everyday challenge of going beyond the broad values that all agree to - to decide what seems right when two or more values conflict. (For example, is it appropriate to lie to avoid hurting someone's feelings? Might it be acceptable to steal to feed one's child?) Rational decisions also determine which rules from the Bible we continue to observe, and which we set aside.

Einstein recognized innate qualities – of cooperation and compassion – that EO Wilson and others feel are rooted in sociobiology. He felt that ethical behavior should be based on our education and our social norms, and he felt it would be a sad statement on our moral character if our ethics were based on fear of punishment from God or the hope for everlasting life as a reward. He said:

> I believe that we have to . . . treat values and moral obligations as a purely human problem - the most important of all human problems.

Albert Einstein. 1947. Hoffmann, p. 95

## Ways of Sensing the Divine

**Everyone who is seriously involved in the pursuit of science**
Albert Einstein. Letter to a child, 1936 (Dukas, p. 32-33)

**Science . . . has confirmed the value of faith**
Clinical studies have shown positive psychological and health outcomes in those who describe themselves as believers
Benson p. 131-132, 174-176

**the presence of things we cannot touch or see**
Fritjof Capra, in his introduction to the Tao of Physics, gave a dramatic description of how a sense of the unperceivable physical world can prompt deep spiritual feelings:
> I was sitting by the ocean one late summer afternoon, watching the waves rolling in and feeling the rhythm of my breathing, when I suddenly became aware of my whole environment as being engaged in a gigantic cosmic dance. Being a physicist, I knew that the sand, rocks, water, and air around me were made of vibrating molecules and atoms, and that these consisted of particles which interacted with one another by creating and destroying other particles. I knew also that the earth's atmosphere was continually bombarded by showers of 'cosmic rays', particles of high energy undergoing multiple collisions as they penetrated the air. All this was familiar to me from my research in high-energy physics, but until that moment I had only experienced it through graphs, diagrams, and mathematical theories. As I sat on that beach my former experiences came to life; I 'saw' cascades of energy coming down from outer space, in which particles were created and destroyed in rhythmic pulses; I 'saw' the atoms of the elements and those of my body participating in this cosmic dance of energy; I felt its rhythm and I 'heard' its sound, and at that moment I knew that this was the Dance of Shiva, the Lord of Dancers worshipped by the Hindus.

**a "spirit" - lies behind and is expressed in all we see**
While he rejected the traditional view of God as a supernatural presence, Einstein nevertheless saw, in the laws of the Universe, something unfathomable and far greater than ourselves. With respect for the order seen in nature, he referred to this, in various statements, as "an intelligence", "a superior reasoning power", and "a spirit vastly superior to that of man". He said:
> If there is any such concept as a God, it is a subtle spirit, not an image of a man that so many have fixed in their minds.
> 
> Albert Einstein. Bucky, p. 86

**these spirits are very real**
> William James described how abstract ideas, such as goodness, beauty, and justice, prompt feelings and actions in those who sense them. He said:
>> We turn towards them and from them, we seek them, hold them, hate them, bless them, just as if they were so many concrete beings. The unseen region in question is not merely ideal, for it produces effects in this world. When we commune with it, work is actually done upon our finite personality, for we are turned into new men, and consequences in the way of conduct follow . . . That which produces effects within another reality must be termed a reality itself . . .
>
> Varieties of Religious Experience, p. 64-65 and 560

**I had the sense that I was intimately connected to everything**
> Anthony Newberg. Why We Believe What We Believe, p. 215-216; quoted from "Kevin"

**We may hear a voice, or have a vision**
> Daniel Smith, p. 6-8

**I experience a happiness that is impossible in an ordinary state**
> Fyodor Dostoevsky; from "The Idiot"

**stimulation of certain brain areas can trigger perceptions**
> Julian Jaynes, p 108-111

**there came a firm, distinct loud voice**
> Julian Jaynes, p 86

**I do think that it is similar to what was heard**
> Julian Jaynes, p 86

**experiencing them is just like hearing an actual sound**
> Julian Jaynes, p 86

**if God exists and speaks to us - we receive a message**
> Newberg, A. Why God Won't Go Away, p. 36-37

**Researchers have identified areas of the brain**
> Newberg, A. Why God Won't Go Away, Chapter 1

**Optical illusions**
> Adapted from images shown in Newberg, A. Why We Believe What We Believe, p. 50 + 54

# A Choice

**The main source of the present-day conflicts**
  Albert Einstein. Science, Philosophy, and Religion, 1941
    (Ideas and Opinions, p. 50)
**non-overlapping magesteria (NOMA)**
  Stephen Jay Gould. Natural History, 1997
**Cardinal Baronius's statement**
  GS Johnson. The Galileo Affair
**The scientific method can teach us nothing else**
  Albert Einstein. From an address at Princeton, 1939
    (Ideas and Opinions, p. 45)
**science without religion is lame**
  Albert Einstein. Science, Philosophy and Religion, 1941
    (Ideas and Opinions, p. 48-49)
**One is 'the way of the kitten"**
  Joseph Campbell. Myths to Live By, p. 129
**My religion consists of a humble admiration**
  Albert Einstein. Bucky, p. 86
**I believe in Spinoza's God**
  Albert Einstein. Telegram to a Jewish newspaper, 1929
    (Calaprice, p. 204)
**Secular Humanism**
  American Humanist Association website
**I am, of course, and have always been an atheist**
  Albert Einstein. Letter to Guy H. Raner, July, 1945
**the idea of a personal God is a childlike one**
  Albert Einstein. Letter to Guy H. Raner, September, 1949
**Taoist quotes**
  Hua Hu Ching (Brian Walker translation)
    #6, #22
  Tao to Ching (Stephen Mitchell translation)
    #4, #6, #14, #25, #37, #51
  Wen Tzu (Thomas Cleary translation)
    #1, #72

## A New Kind of Faith

**Try and penetrate with our limited means the secrets of nature**
    Albert Einstein. From a conversation with Harry Kessler (Brian, p. 161)

**Hindu text - a scene on a battlefield at dawn**
    Bhagavad Gita

**By asking, they receive . . .**
    Through prayer . . . things which cannot be realized in any other manner come about: energy which but for prayer would be bound is by prayer set free . . .
    William James. Varieties of Religious Experience, p. 507

**strength to deal with problems**
    George Gallup. Public Perspective, May/June 2000, p. 15

**tap hidden reserves of faith and courage**
    Harold Kushner, When Bad Things Happen, p. 125

**you didn't get a miracle to avert a tragedy**
    Harold Kushner, When Bad Things Happen, p. 131

**prayer does not change God**
    Attributed to Soren Kierkegaard

**prayer can offer an increased sense of well-being**
    Masters, p. 334
    American Cancer Society website. Spirituality and Prayer

**meditation . . . is clearly relaxing**
    Herbert Benson, p. 131-132

**quiet the mind and the body**
    Herbert Benson, p. 213

**faith . . . a trusting acceptance of God's will**
    American Heritage Dictionary

**common ideals - in different cultures and times**
    As is shown in the book, Oneness, by Jeffrey Moses, the Golden Rule is present, with different wording, in all faiths. And many other values (honor your parents, seek wisdom, find contentment, be charitable, persevere, etc.) are seen in major religions.

**the Good, the True, and the Beautiful in humanity**
    Albert Einstein. Ideas and Opinions, p. 52

**I believe in the brotherhood of man**
    Clark, p. 622

**God is a symbol**
> In a written response to Einstein's rejection of a personal God (1940) the theologian, Paul Tillich described God as "a symbol, not an object, and it never should be interpreted as an object." But, he also felt that, as a focus for a sense of connection and a means of envisioning what is holy, "the symbol of the personal God is indispensable for living religion."
>
> Jammer, p. 109-112

William James expressed a similar view, when he said:
> Immanuel Kant held a curious doctrine about such objects of belief as God, the design of creation, the soul, its freedom, and the life hereafter. These things, he said, are properly not objects of knowledge at all. Our conceptions always require a sense-content to work with, and as the words 'soul,' 'God,' 'immortality,' cover no distinctive sense-content whatever, it follows that theoretically speaking they are words devoid of any significance. Yet strangely enough they have a definite meaning for our practice. We can act as if there were a God; feel as if we were free; consider Nature as if she were full of special designs; lay plans as if we were to be immortal; and we find then that these words do make a genuine difference in our moral life. Our faith that these unintelligible objects actually exist proves thus to be a full equivalent . . ., from the point of view of our action, for a knowledge of what they might be . . . So we have the strange phenomenon . . . of a mind believing with all its strength in the real presence of a set of things of no one of which it can form any notion whatsoever.
>
> Varieties of Religious Experience, p. 64

And, in keeping with his sense of ideas as "real" (discussed earlier), he said:
> God is real since he produces real effects.
>
> Varieties of Religious Experience, p. 561

**all that happens makes sense as part of a larger plan**
> Einstein, himself, expressed this view a week before his death. When he seemed to be in pain and was asked if everything was comfortable, he replied:
>> "Everything is comfortable, but I am not."
>>
>> Brian, p. 424

**believers had better health outcomes**
Herbert Benson 174-176
**took control over what I could and gave the rest up to God**
Harold Koenig, p. 123
**it does not matter which God you worship**
Herbert Benson, Timeless Healing, p. 212
**You become a certain kind of person**
Harold Kushner, Who Needs God?, p. 34

## A New Kind of Religion

**A religion . . . that stressed the magnificence of the universe**
Carl Sagan. Pale Blue Dot, p. 52
**new kind of religion**
Albert Einstein. Letter to Hans Muehsam, March, 1954 (Calaprice, p. 218)
**an active relationship with the unseen power**
William James. Varieties of Religious Experience, p. 505-6
**all the finer speculations in the realm of science . . .**
Albert Einstein. Science and God: A Dialogue, 1930 (Calaprice 2005, p. 199)
**seek, and you shall find**
Matthew 7:7
**Climb the mountains and get their good tidings**
John Muir. Our National Parks, 1901, page 56.
**all the world seems a church and the mountains altars**
John Muir. My First Summer in the Sierra, 1869. Sept. 7.
**The sense of what one is connecting to may be vague**
The Tao that can be described is not the Tao.
Tao te Ching. Lao Tzu. #1
**Some feel that religion requires the supernatural**
The American Heritage Dictionary defines religion as "Belief in and reverence for a supernatural power or powers"

## Postscript

**With primitive man**
Albert Einstein, NY Times Magazine. November 9, 1930.

# Bibliography

American Cancer Society website. Spirituality and Prayer. http://www.cancer.org/docroot/ETO/content/ETO_5_3X_Spirituality_and_Prayer.asp

American Humanist Association website. www.americanhumanist.org

Benson, Herbert. Timeless Healing: The power and biology of belief. Scribner. NY. 1996.

Brian, Denis. Einstein: A Life. John Wiley & Sons. NY. 1996.

Bucky, Peter. The Private Albert Einstein. Andrews and McMeel, Kansas City, 1992.

Calaprice, Alice (ed.). The Expanded Quotable Einstein. Princeton University Press. Princeton, NJ. 2000.

Calaprice, Alice (ed.). The New Quotable Einstein. Princeton University Press. Princeton, NJ. 2005.

Campbell, Joseph. Myths to Live By. Bantam. NY. 1984.

Capra, Fritjof. The Tao of Physics. Bantam, NY, 1975.

Clark RW. Einstein: The life and times. Harper Perennial. 2007.

Cleary, Thomas (translation). The Taoist Classics. (Volumes 1-2). Shambala. Boston. 1999.

Dawkins, Richard. Unweaving the Rainbow : Science, Delusion, and the Appetite for Wonder. Houghton Mifflin. Boston. 1998.

Dennett, Daniel. Breaking the Spell: Religion as a Natural Phenomenon. Viking. 2006.

Dukas Helen and Hoffman B. (ed.). Albert Einstein - The Human Side. Princeton University Press. 1979.

Einstein, Albert. Ideas and Opinions. Modern Library. NY. 1994. (originally by Crown Publishers in 1954)

Einstein, Albert. The World As I See It. Philosophical Library. NY. 1949.

Einstein, Albert. Science and Religion. New York Times Magazine. November 9, 1930:1-4.

Einstein, Albert. Autobiographical Notes. (Schilpp PA, ed.). Open Court. 1991.

Gallup, George. Keeping the Faith. Public Perspective. May/June 2000.

Gould, Stephen Jay, "Nonoverlapping Magisteria," Natural History 106 (March 1997):16-22.

Hoffmann B. Albert Einstein: Creator and Rebel. Plume. 1973.

Isaacson, Walter. Einstein. Simon & Schuster. NY. 2007.

James W. Varieties of Religious Experience. 1902. Modern Library 1994 edition.

Johnston GS. The Galileo Affair. Catholic.net website. http://www.catholic.net/rcc/Periodicals/Issues/GalileoAffair.html

Jammer Max. Einstein and Religion. Princeton University Press. 1999.

Jaynes, Julian. The Origin of Consciousness. Houghton Mifflin. Boston. 1976.

Koenig H and McConnell M. The Healing Power of Faith: How Belief and Prayer Can Help You Triumph Over Disease. Simon & Schuster. NY. 2001.

Kushner, Harold. When Bad Things Happen to Good People. Schocken Books, NY. 1981.

Kushner, Harold. Who Needs God. Summit Books, NY. 1989.

Meade, CA. Feynman as a Colleague. In Feynman and Computation. Hey, Anthony (ed.) Westview Press. Cambridge, MA. 2002.

Mitchell, Stephen (translation). Tao te Ching. Harper Perennial. NY. 1991.

Moses, Jeffrey. Oneness. Ballentine, NY. 1989.

Muir, John. Our National Parks. 1901.

Muir, John. My First Summer in the Sierra. 1869.

Newberg Andrew. D'Aquili E, and Rause V. Why God Won't Go Away. Ballentine. NY. 2001.

Newberg, Andrew. Why We Believe What We Believe. Free Press. NY. 2006.

Powell, Corey. God in the Equation: How Einstein Became the Prophet of the New Religious Era. Free Press. NY. 2002.

Raner, Guy. Einstein on His Personal Religious Views. Freethought Today Vol. 21 No. 9. 2004.

Rosenkranz Z. The Einstein Scrapbook. Johns Hopkins University Press, 2002.

Sagan, Carl. Pale Blue Dot. Random House. NY. 1994.

Sagan, Carl. The Varieties of Scientific Experience. Penguin. 2006.

Shermer, Michael. How We Believe: The Search for God in an Age of Science. W.H. Freeman, NY. 2000.

Smith, Daniel. Muses, Madmen, and Prophets: Rethinking the History, Science, and Meaning of Auditory Hallucination. Penguin. NY. 2007.

Walker, Brian (translation). Hua Hu Ching. HarperCollins, NY. 1995.

Wilson Edward O. On Human Nature. Bantam, NY, 1979.

Wilson Edward O. The Future of Life. Knopf. NY. 2002.

www.ingramcontent.com/pod-product-compliance
Lightning Source LLC
Chambersburg PA
CBHW030004050426
42451CB00006B/110